A Safe Home for Shanti Cow

A Safe Home for Shanti Cow
By Linda Voith

A Safe Home for Shanti Cow

Govinda Goshala Cow Haven
7326 Gleason Hill Road
Belfast, NY 14711
govindagoshala.org

Formatting: Deepak Gupta (fiverr.com/weformat)
Production & Layout: Shalini Bosbyshell (kailashdesign.com)

Govinda Goshala
Cow Haven

Dear Reader: If you enjoy this book, please share it with your friends, place it in your local library, or get involved by becoming a goshala member. By spreading the word, you can help ensure a future in which more cows will be able to live their lives in a loving and safe home.

ISBN: 978-1-7328469-0-6
LCCN: 2018911682

Names: Voith, Linda, author. | Tytka, Gilly, photographer.
Title: A safe home for shanti cow / Linda Voith ; [photographs by] Gilly Tytka.
Description: Belfast, NY : Govinda Goshala Cow Haven, 2018.
Identifiers: LCCN 2018911682 | ISBN 978-1-7328469-0-6 (paperback) | ISBN 978-1-7328469-2-0 (hardcover) | ISBN 978-1-7328469-1-3 (ebook)
Subjects: LCSH: Animal sanctuaries--Juvenile literature. | Animal welfare--Juvenile literature. | CYAC: Cows. | Animals--Treatment. | Emotions in animals. | BISAC: JUVENILE NONFICTION / Animals / Cows. | JUVENILE NONFICTION / Animals / Animal Welfare.
Classification: LCC HV4708 .V65 2018 (print) | LCC HV4708 (ebook) | DDC 179/.3--dc23.

To all the young people in my life who helped get the dreams out of my head and into a form where they could be lived and shared.

and

To my husband Stephen, whose hard work and dedication made it possible for Shanti, Bella, Chintamani and all of their babies to have a safe home.

Shanti is a milk cow who grew up on a dairy farm. She lived outside all of her life with lots of friends.

Every morning Shanti and her friends waited eagerly for Farmer Janice to call them into the barn for milking.

Shanti and her friends loved to come into the barn because that is where they ate their hay and grain. Shanti loved to eat. She was always hungry.

One day, Farmer Janice noticed that she was running low on feed. "There is not enough hay to last through the winter," she said.

4

"We are going to have to sell some of our cows. Shanti is my favorite. How can we find a safe home for her?" Farmer Janice wondered.

"I will call Linda and Steve at the Goshala. They love cows. Maybe they can give Shanti a good home with their other cows," she said.

Linda quickly called her friends and asked them to donate some money to help save Shanti. Everyone helped. "It only takes a little when everyone works together," said Linda.

When Shanti arrived at the Goshala she was very
quiet. She missed her friends at the dairy farm.
Steve brushed Shanti and tried to make her feel
at home.

Shanti was giving five gallons of milk every day. Linda milked Shanti so that her udder would not get too full. She fed Shanti lots and lots of hay, because Shanti was always hungry.

The other cows came to visit. Shanti liked her new friends, but she was still homesick.

"Shanti is pregnant," said Linda. "Her new baby won't be born for a long time. Lets adopt a calf for Shanti, maybe that will cheer her up."

So Linda and Steve went back to Farmer Janice's dairy farm where they saw 25 little calves. They were all so cute. Linda wanted them all. "No," said Steve, "there are only two of us to care for them. At least we can take one."

"Take this one," said Farmer Janice, "she is Shanti's granddaughter." Little Sharah was brown with a white lightning stripe. She rode home in the car on Linda's lap.

Steve carried Sharah into the barn and lifted her over the door of Shanti's stall. Shanti quietly sniffed at Sharah. Then, all of a sudden, Shanti got excited.

Shanti sniffed and sniffed Sharah all over. Then Shanti licked and licked Sharah all over, until she was soaking wet.

Little Sharah snuggled next to Shanti and drank her warm milk. Shanti was HAPPY! She loves babies.

After Sharah was done drinking milk she began to walk. She was wobbly. She had never had a chance to walk around before. She had always lived in a small pen.

Sharah walked... then she jumped... and then she ran. She ran back and forth... and back and forth... and back and forth. Running was fun!

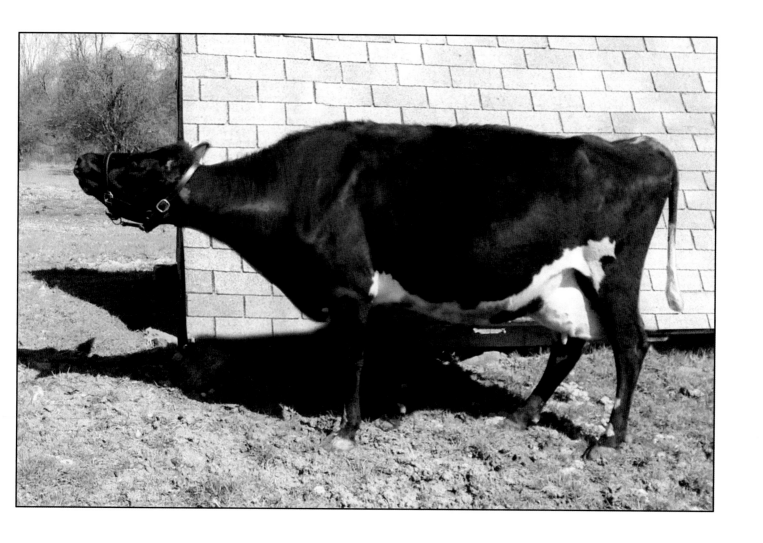

Shanti was upset. She wanted Sharah to stay close to her. "Come back. Come back," Shanti mooed.

After a while of running around, little Sharah was all tired out. She curled up with her grandmother and went to sleep.

In the morning Shanti wanted to go outside to eat the soft green spring grass. Shanti loved to eat. She was always hungry.

Little Sharah was not interested in eating grass. She was having too much fun running around the big pasture. Shanti ran all around the pasture too, trying to keep up with Sharah to make sure she was safe.

22

Shanti was so upset that she could not eat in peace. So Linda put Sharah into a special pen where Shanti could see her. Little Sharah could run and play with the goats, but she could not run too far away from Shanti.

When Shanti saw that little Sharah was safe, she finally settled down and ate her grass peacefully. Shanti was hungry after all of that running around.

Steve wanted to play with Sharah and the goats
too. He pretended to be a calf eating grass. Shanti
and all the goats thought he was crazy!

One rainy morning, Shanti hid underneath some big trees to stay dry and that is where her calf, Krishi, was born.

Shanti loved to watch her babies grow. Sharah and Krishi played together every day. At night they snuggled with Shanti and went to sleep.

Shanti is finally peaceful now that she has two calves to love.

You can help cows like Shanti and her friends have a safe home. You can help by feeding cows... because cows are always hungry.

More About Cows

There are two things that cows love best in all the world. They love to nurse their babies and to eat green grass.

Cows can eat 40 pounds of food every day. Cows favorite food is green grass. In winter they will eat hay (dried grass), but they don't enjoy it as much. Cows can drink 30-50 gallons of water every day.

A cow's milk bag is called an udder. The udder is where a cow produces milk. Cows on dairy farms give 7-8 gallons of milk each day. Calves grow into full grown cows by 2-3 years old.

Here is a picture of Shanti at the Goshala with her two babies, now all grown up. A Goshala is a type of cow sanctuary that originated in India, where cows are celebrated as a living symbol of Mother Nature. Goshalas provide lifetime care and shelter for cows.

If you would like to get involved or make an online donation to help change the lives of cows in the USA, please visit us at:

govindagoshala.org
Govinda Goshala Cow Haven

If you would like to make a contribution to help care for the cows at the goshala, you can mail this form to us at:

Govinda Goshala Cow Haven
7326 Gleason Hill Road
Belfast, NY 14711

☐ $5 will buy one square bale of hay that will feed a cow for a day

☐ $10 will buy a brush to groom the cows

☐ $25 will buy a bottle of neem oil to keep flies away from the cows

☐ $50 will buy a large round bale of hay that will feed the whole herd for one day

☐ $108 toward veterinary expenses

☐ $_____ other amount

☐ $_____ monthly contribution

Any amount helps. Thank you!

Made in the USA
Middletown, DE
26 June 2019